CHARING CROSS TO DARTFORD

Vic Mitchell and Keith Smith

Middleton Press

The view from Charing Cross signal box on Saturday 3rd
January 1959 includes trains from Bromley North (10),
Slade Green via Lewisham and Woolwich (60), Dartford
via Bexleyheath (70) and Dartford via Greenwich and
Woolwich (80). (R.C.Riley)

First published March 1990

ISBN 0 906520 75 4

© Middleton Press 1990

Design and Laser typesetting -
        Deborah Goodridge

Published by Middleton Press
            Easebourne Lane
            Midhurst, West Sussex
            GU29 9AZ
            Tel. (0730) 813169

Printed & bound by Biddles Ltd,
        Guildford and Kings Lynn

CONTENTS

ACKNOWLEDGEMENTS

We are very grateful to many of the photographers mentioned in the captions and to R.M.Casserley, R.Randell, Dr.E.Course, G.Croughton, N.Langridge and N.Stanyon for assistance so generously given. As usual, our wives have been of immeasurable help.

GEOGRAPHICAL SETTING

Most of the route traverses the flood plain alluvium and gravels of the lower Thames Valley but, in the Woolwich area, it was built on or tunnelled through Thanet Sand. Thames tributaries crossed include the Ravensbourne River east of Deptford, the River Cray south of Slade Green and the River Darent at Dartford.

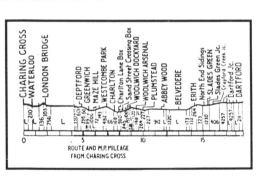

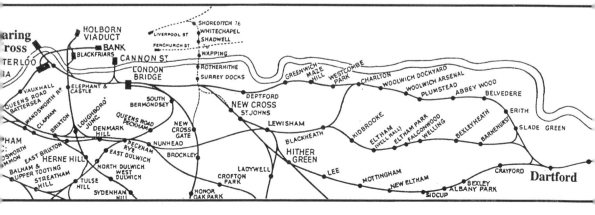

HISTORICAL BACKGROUND

The London and Greenwich Railway's Act was passed on 17th May 1833 and, being London's first railway, some of its unusual details are worth considering. The entire double track route was built on a series of 878 brick arches, each of 18ft span, 28ft wide and about 22 ft high. This remarkable engineering feat involved laying bricks at the rate of 100,000 each day. They were made near Sittingbourne and bought by barge to a wharf on the Surrey Canal.

The line was bought into use between Deptford and Spa Road on 8th February 1836, the service being extended to London Bridge on 14th December 1836. Before arrival at the termini, the locomotive of each train was uncoupled at speed by one of the guards; it was run into one of the two platforms; the points were changed smartly and the train was diverted into the adjacent platform. The management had no experience of railway operation and the only staff with any had been poached from the Liverpool and Manchester Railway.

Extension from Deptford to a temporary terminus at Church Row, Greenwich, took place on 24th December 1838. The permanent station was not available until 12th April 1840.

Among the unusual features of the Act was that individual parishes would specify what materials were to be used for the construction of bridges over streets in their area. Another clause allowed the railway to construct a toll path beside their viaduct - this was to prove to be a valuable source of revenue, although the charge was only 1d per person. Less successful was the proposed leasing of the damp arches as dwellings. The infant railway was soon very busy with both commercial and recreational traffic. The latter included crowds visiting Greenwich Park, the waterfront and the regular fair at Greenwich.

The Government saw no need for other railway routes into South London and so insisted that the London and Croydon and the London and Brighton operated their trains over L&G tracks to the terminus at London Bridge, paying a toll when so doing. Trains from Croydon joined at Corbetts Lane Junction from 5th June 1839 and the L&BR services commenced on the same route on 12th July 1841. The L&CR and the L&BR were amalgamated on 26th July 1846 to form the London, Brighton and South Coast Railway.

The South Eastern Railway was obliged to use the LBSCR route to London Bridge for their trains form Dover and Folkestone, which joined the line at what is now Redhill.

The SER leased the L&GR from 1845 (technically until 1923) and so further development of the North Kent line was under its control. Owing to objections from the Admiralty, the Vicar of Greenwich and others it was not possible to continue the L&G line under Greenwich Park to Woolwich, although the Royal Observatory gained sufficient concessions to withdraw its objections. The North Kent route from Dartford was therefore diverted south at Charlton to run through a long tunnel to Blackheath and then to turn north again at Lewisham. It rejoined the old L&G tracks at North Kent East Junction. Traffic began on 30th July 1849, when a through service from "Rochester" (now Strood) and Gravesend commenced.

The freight only branch to Angerstein Wharf came into use in 1852 and Lewisham became a junction in 1857, when the route to Beckenham was opened. The Dartford Loop, via Bexley, followed in 1866, the next development in the area being the opening of the one mile long branch from Charlton to Maze Hill, on 1st January 1873. The connection between Maze Hill and Greenwich finally opened on 1st February 1878, more than forty years after it had been proposed as part of a London to Dover Railway.

The Bexleyheath line was the third route between London and Dartford and was ready for traffic on 1st May 1895, nearly half a century after the North Kent trains started to run through Dartford.

Developments in the country had brought a vast increase in traffic at London Bridge which was partially eased by the opening by the SER of a West End terminus at Charing Cross on 11th January 1864 and a City terminus at Cannon Street on 1st September 1866. Between the two, a connection with the London, Chatham & Dover Railway's line to Blackfriars and the Metropolitan Railway was opened on 1st June 1878, diverging at Metropolitan Junction.

Third rail electrification of all routes between Charing Cross and Dartford took place in 1926. Some trains commenced on 10th May but, owing to a miners' strike, the full service did not commence until 19th July.

PASSENGER SERVICES

One train an hour was provided initially between Dartford and Spa Road and this was increased to a 30 minute interval service from May 1836, when Sunday trains were also introduced. Upon opening to London Bridge in December of that year, the interval was reduced to 15 minutes. Even this remarkable frequency was insufficient at peak times, such as Greenwich Fair days, when trains were run as often as possible. From March 1839, the interval was twenty minutes, reduced to ten minutes in the six peak hours.

Initially a half-hourly service was provided between Woolwich and London Bridge, with a small number originating at Dartford or beyond. From 1866 until 1916, most North Kent trains to and from Charing Cross ran via Cannon Street.

By 1869, the weekday timetable was showing 39 trains to Woolwich, of which 26 continued to Dartford or beyond. The Sunday figures were 23 and 11 respectively.

When Maze Hill opened in 1873, a shuttle service of 12 trains to Charlton was operated, half of them continuing to Woolwich Arsenal.

From June 1878, a regular service between Finsbury Park and Woolwich Arsenal via Farringdon was operated. It was later extended to Enfield but was discontinued in May 1907, by which time the electrified tramways were having a competitive effect.

Frequency on the North Kent Line continued to increase, with a number of peak hour trains terminating at Maze Hill or Erith.

Electrification to Dartford in 1926 gave a basic half-hourly service through Blackheath and Woolwich, in addition to the longer distance steam trains. Greenwich had a London - Plumstead service every 30 minutes. Extension of electric traction to Gravesend in 1930 resulted in two North Kent trains per hour terminating there. After wartime curtailments, the basic service in 1948 comprised two trains per hour to Dartford via Greenwich, one via Blackheath and one fast (every other hour) to Gillingham, calling only at Woolwich Arsenal, between London Bridge and Dartford. Ten years later, the timetable was similar, but with two via Blackheath, hourly. With the extension of electrification to the Kent Coast in 1959 the Gillingham service (by then hourly) was extended to Margate via Faversham, but it was cut back to Gillingham again in May 1986.

FINSBURY PARK, KING'S CROSS, LONDON BRIDGE, and WOOLWICH.—G. N. & S. E.

(1890 timetable — passenger service between Finsbury Park, King's Cross, London Bridge and Woolwich)

1890

LONDON, GREENWICH, and WOOLWICH.—South Eastern.

Charing Cross to Greenwich & Woolwich at 6 12, 7, 7 28, 8, 8 22, 8 42, 9, 9 20, 9 42, 10 2, 10 20, *10 40, 11 2, *11 20, and 11 40 mrn.; *12 noon; 12 20, 12 42, 1, *1 20, 1 42, 2, 2 22, *2 40, 3, *3 20, 3 42, *4, 4 20, 4 42, 5 2, 5 20, 5 40, 6, 6 22, 6 40, 7 2, 7 22, 7 40, 8, 8 30, 9 2, *9¼, 10, 10½, 11 2, *11 13 (from London Bridge, and 11¼ aft.; *12 2 night. SUNDAYS at 8½, 9½, and 10½ mrn., 12½, 1, 1½, 2, 2½, 3, 3½, 4, 4½, 5, 5½, 6, 6½, 7, and half-hourly to 11½ aft.

Woolwich Arsenal to Greenwich and Charing Cross at 6½, 7 20, 7 40, 8 20, 8 40, 9, 9 20, 10, 10 20, 10 40, 11, & 11 20 mrn.; 12 noon; 12 40, 1 20, 1 40, 2, 40, 3 20, †3 45, 4, 4 40, 5 20, 5 40, 6, 6 20, 6 40, 7, 7 20, 7 55, 8 25, 8 55, 9 25, 9 55, 10 20, 10 55, and 11 25 aft. SUNDAYS at 6 50, 8 10, 9 10, & 10 10 mrn., and every half-hour from 12 10 to 11 10 aft.

Extra.—Greenwich to Charing Cross at 8 5 and 8 49 mrn. not stopping at Cannon Street. Maze Hill to Greenwich and Charing Cross at †5 17, 6 5, 7 12, †7½, †7 48, †8 27, †and 11 53 mrn.; 12 33, 1 13, 2 33, 3 13, ‡ 53, 4 33, and 5 13 aft.

* To Maze Hill only. † To Cannon Street only ‡ To London Bridge only.

CHARING CROSS

1. The station was opened with six platforms on 11th January 1864 but this splendid arched roof collapsed on 5th December 1905. Its progressive failure gave time to evacuate passengers, stop an incoming train and for all but two painters working on the roof to escape. There were other fatalities in a nearby theatre on which one of the walls collapsed. (National Railway Museum)

The 1895 map has Charing Cross station on the left and the LSWR Waterloo terminus on the right, with seven tracks converging to three at the east end of the bridge. A turntable was added later, south of Sutton Street.

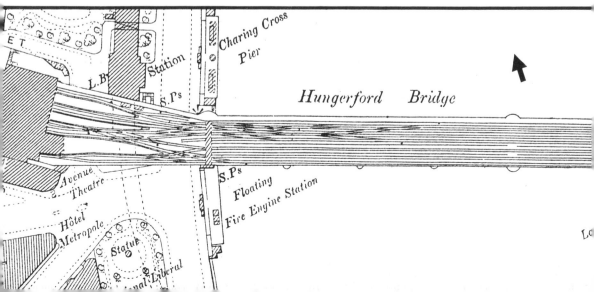

2. The bridge replaced Brunel's Hungerford Suspension Bridge, which was dismantled and used in the construction of the present bridge over the Clifton Gorge at Bristol. In 1884 the bridge was widened to take seven tracks and the footway on the right (upstream side) was lost, the other one still being in use today. (D.Cullum coll.)

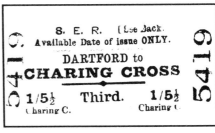

S. E. R.   (See Back.
Available Date of issue ONLY.

DARTFORD to
CHARING CROSS

1/5½   Third.   1/5½
Charing C.   Charing C.

3. The SER's Charing Cross Hotel was built above the main entrance to the station and was opened in May 1865. The hotel had nearly 300 rooms and almost as many employees but the clientele changed somewhat when Continental traffic was concentrated on Victoria in 1920.

The stone cross in the forecourt was also erected in 1865 and is a replica of the 1295 Eleanor Cross, which was built in memory of the wife of King Edward I.
(National Railway Museum)

S. E. & C. R. (SEE BACK)
Available Day of issue ONLY.

Cannon Street to

CHARING CROSS

Revised Fare   Revised Fare
7d   First Class   **7d**
Charing Cross   Charing Cross

5. Lattice girders flanked a single track which had two lines to the south of it and four to the north. Class D1 no.1502 passes over the Victoria Embankment on 30th September 1938. This part of the bridge was severely damaged by enemy action on 18th June 1944.
(H.C.Casserley)

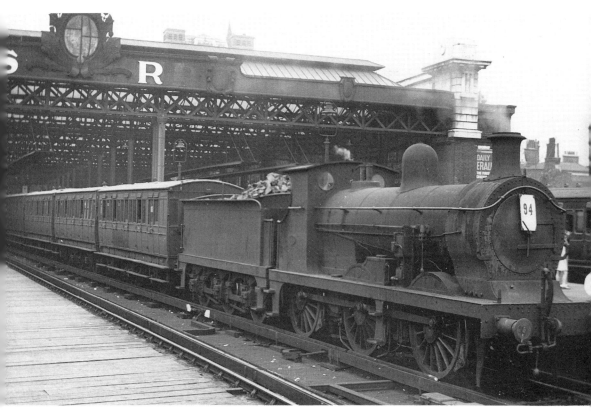

4. The 1906 roof originally carried the letters SECR and that company's crest. A photograph taken on 5th August 1933 reveals that six-wheeled coaches were still in use at a time when most local services were electrically operated. The headcode is London - Addiscombe, but the stock might be for an excursion. (H.F.Wheeller)

6. The rear of the Charing Cross Hotel and the signal box are seen in March 1955. The latter remained in use until 16th April 1976, having controlled colour light signals since 27th June 1926. In 1989, £3m was spent on modernising the station. (R.C.Riley)

7. The wrought iron of the original part of the bridge was replaced in 1979, necessitating closure of platforms 1 - 3 for about six months. The upstream part had been extensively rebuilt in 1948. In May 1989, we see one of the most expensive sidings in London, together with the main buildings of Waterloo station, by then the lowest on the skyline. (A.Mott)

9. Another view from the main offices at Waterloo shows the continuation of the lines from Charing Cross and the four platforms of Waterloo East. The canopy and valance (lower right) were once adjacent to a line connecting the LSWR and the SER stations. They were removed in 1986 to make way for small shops to be built adjacent to the footway connecting the two stations. (J.Scrace)

8. The rear coaches of the 3.25pm Charing Cross to Hastings pass the Royal Festival Hall on 29th September 1955, while the leading ones are over York Road. Behind 4-4-0 no. 30926 *Repton* is the Shot Tower, once used for the production of gun shot by allowing drops of molten lead to solidify while dropping into a water tank at the base of the tower. (D.Cullum)

WATERLOO EAST

10. Opened as Waterloo Junction on 1st January 1869, the name was changed to Waterloo Eastern on 7th July 1935 and officially became "East" on 2nd May 1977. Unit no. 1466 displays T for Addiscombe on 17th October 1929. (H.C.Casserley)

11. Class B1 4-4-0 no. 1441 nears the end of its journey on 24th February 1939, as it passes over Eaton Street. The up and down local lines had been reversed between Charing Cross and Metropolitan Junction on 24th August 1925. The headcode indicates the North Kent and Greenwich route. (H.C.Casserley)

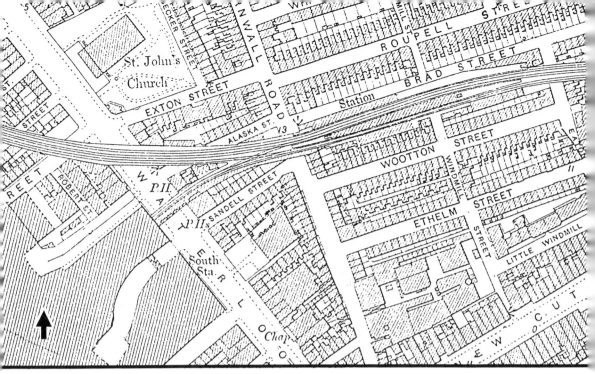

This map is continuous with the previous one and marks the single line connection between the SER and LSWR, passing over Waterloo Road. South Station refers to part of the complicated arrangement of the old terminus, which is explained in the companion albums, *Waterloo to Woking* and *Waterloo to Windsor*.

12. No. 34081 *92 Squadron* stands at platform C on 1st August 1957, with the 1.8pm "Man of Kent" from Charing Cross, while renovation work proceeds in the background. The platforms are lettered A to D, to avoid confusion with the 21 terminal platforms in the main station. (D.Cullum)

13. During the reconstruction of Hungerford Bridge in 1979-80, a temporary additional footbridge was provided, from which this photograph was taken. Trains terminated at platforms A and B, using the scissors crossover seen beyond the signals. A train to Blackfriars crosses the former LCDR bridge in the distance, Blackfriars Road station being situated this side of the bridge until 1869. (D.Clayton)

15. An eastward view from Metropolitan Junction box in 1979 shows the line to Cannon Street curving to the left and those to London Bridge in the centre. It is this short length of double track over Borough Market which creates a serious bottleneck for traffic and which again is subject to a quadrupling proposal. Southwark Cathedral is in the background and the Hop Exchange is on the right. (British Rail)

METROPOLITAN JUNCTION

14. The name originated from the fact that the spur linked the SER with the Metropolitan Extension of the LCDR. The up local line is occupied by an EMU from Dartford (via Bexleyheath) as a special train descends the steep spur from the Blackfriars line on 18th April 1960. Passenger services on this line were resumed in May 1988, after an interval of over 70 years, although an early morning newspaper train did carry passengers for some years. (A.E.Bennett)

SOUTHWARK DEPOT

16. The Southwark Depot (pronounced Suthuk) is seen from a train bound for Blackfriars. The Ewer Street Depot locomotive coaling crane is on the right but the adjacent turntable is not visible. Engines ceased to use these facilities upon completion of the Kent electrification in 1961. (A.E.Bennett)

The 1873 survey has the Charing Cross line on the left and shows the LCDR passing over it. The "Timber Yard" and "Iron Works" in Ewer Street were acquired for the construction of a continental freight depot and a locomotive servicing area, which included a 55ft turntable. The Cannon Street and London Bridge lines diverged over the tram tracks of Southwark Street, on the right.

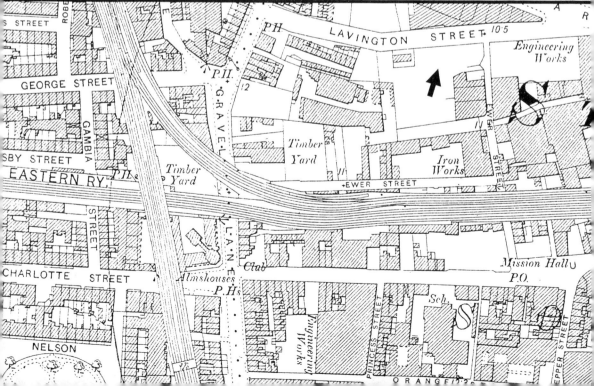

17. The entrance in Great Suffolk Street (Gravel Lane on the 1873 map) still bore the carved words GRAND VITESSE GOODS DEPOT, when photographed in 1965. The period road signs are seen from Dolben Street, formerly George Street. (J.J.Smith)

CANNON STREET

18. E.M.Barry designed the frontage of what was for sometime known as the City Terminus Hotel. This was eventually converted to offices and named Southern House but was largely destroyed during the last war. The Metropolitan and District Railway's entrance is in the foreground.
(National Railway Museum)

19. Hawkshaw's bold roof and massive towers were an impressive statement to the City that the SER had arrived. About 27 million bricks were laid prior to the opening on 1st September 1866. Ex-LCDR class M3 no. 485 stands over the Thames, alongside the lightweight platforms. (Lens of Sutton)

An incident in 1940 recounted in *War on the Line* reprinted by Middleton Press in 1984.

The scene must now be shifted temporarily to London Bridge on the night of December 9th, when an enemy landmine came down by parachute. It did not go off but mysteriously festooned itself round a signal box close to the station. A bomb is a matter for the Army, but a landmine on an apparently perverse principle for the Navy, and a message was sent to the Admiralty accordingly. Meanwhile, the station was entirely evacuated, only the Stationmaster remaining at his post. The two signalmen perfectly understanding their extreme danger, stayed in their box for two hours in order to clear the line. With the morning light arrived two young naval officers, who inspected the mine and then came back to the station. The senior of them wrote down the course he proposed to take in order that if he did not come back somebody else should be left possessing at least the negative knowledge of what not to do. Then, bidding his subordinate stay behind, he set out again on his walk down the platform, his steps making the only sound in that ghostly station till they died away and those left behind waited in complete silence. Presently the steps were heard returning ; the mine had been made harmless ; the station was re-opened, and of all the crowds of daily travellers that poured in by their daily trains not one knew anything of the deadly drama which had lately been played there. If that mine had exploded, London Bridge Station would for a long time for all practical purposes have ceased to exist.

The bombing year ended with the famous fire raid of December

29th, which so devastated the City of London and on this night London Bridge was in the centre of the picture. At six o'clock came the yellow warning, five minutes later came purple, and at 6.9 red. Half an hour of waiting and then showers of incendiaries over the station and forecourt. The fire squad with other members of the staff helped by police and troops put them all out, but meanwhile large business houses in a street nearby caught fire, and the flames spread towards the station. They might have been kept away by the firefighters, but a bomb had hit the water mains and the water failed. The Fire Brigade and the Station Fire Squad tried to get water from the river, but it was low tide and not till 12 o'clock could any effective pressure be obtained. By that time it was too late ; the fire had a firm grip and was beyond control. A quarter of an hour later a large factory collapsed in flames on the line, and it was feared that the fire might reach the timbers of the railway bridge.

This was prevented by the water from an engine in the station used through a stirrup pump. That was one bright spot ; so was the fact that empty stock was successfully moved into safety. Through the timely moving of all save those who could directly help there was not a single casualty, and most wonderful of all, the train service, though curtailed, never wholly ceased to function, for the trains from Charing Cross and Cannon Street still ran from a single platform. But the material damage was very severe, including the offices of seven departments entirely wiped out.

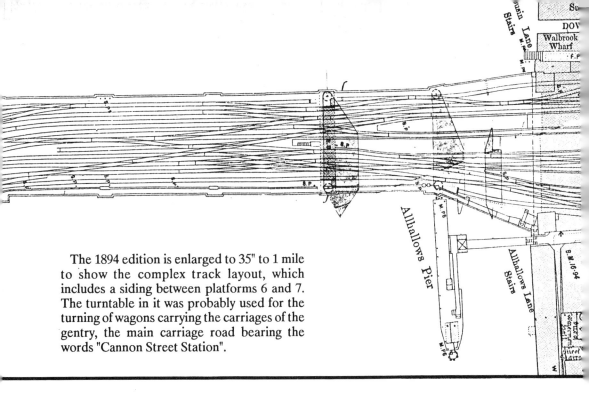

The 1894 edition is enlarged to 35" to 1 mile to show the complex track layout, which includes a siding between platforms 6 and 7. The turntable in it was probably used for the turning of wagons carrying the carriages of the gentry, the main carriage road bearing the words "Cannon Street Station".

20. The massive signal box could be extremely busy owing to the reversal of most Charing Cross trains and the need to handle so many light engine movements. Reversals diminished during WWI and largely ceased with the advent of suburban electrification in 1926. The station was closed from 5th to 26th June of that year, to permit track alterations. (Lens of Sutton)

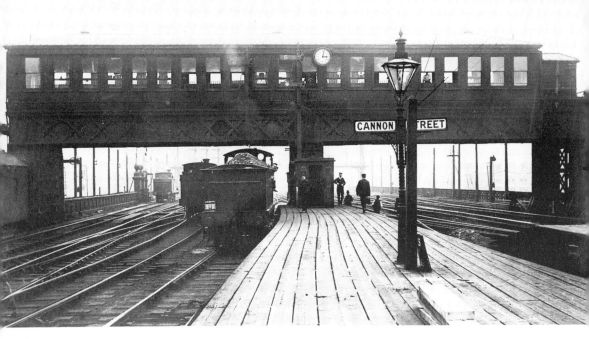

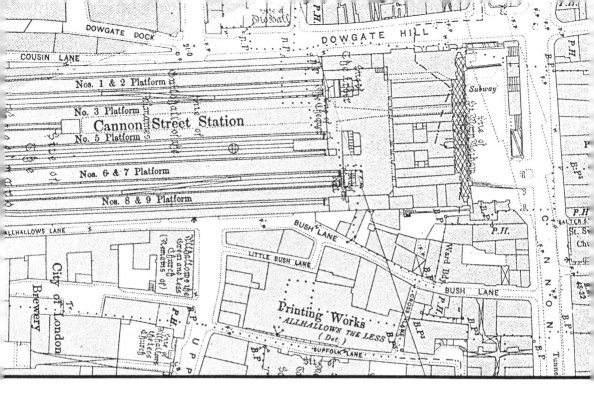

21. Platform canopies were erected following the loss of the roof glazing during WWII. They are seen in this 1954 photograph, which also shows the ticket barriers before the platforms were lengthened to accommodate 10-coach trains. (R.C.Riley)

22. Cars are parked on a bomb site as we marvel at the audacity of the Victorians who erected over 1000 tons of steel to form a train shed. In 1892, the bridge was widened to take ten tracks. The signal box presents its back to us as the 6.3pm service to Hastings departs on 17th May 1956. (J.J.Smith)

24. A bomb scar is evident above the colour light signals (introduced in 1926), as class L1 4-4-0 no. 31786 waits to leave at 4.31 pm for Ramsgate via Faversham, on Friday 12th June 1959. It was the last day that this service was steam worked. (J.H.Aston)

23. Early on 5th April 1957, a serious fire in the relay room of the signal box caused closure of the station. Part of the box was retained and was quickly fitted with a 47 lever frame from Crewe. This enabled some electric services to be resumed on 5th May. Work on dismantling the roof structure was carried out between the rush hours and at the weekends. The progress was recorded on 5th September 1958. (J.H.Aston)

25. The temporary signal box was replaced by this box which was built south of the river, on the site of the approach to the old engine shed. It came into use on 15th December 1957 and is seen in April 1976, just prior to its closure. (J.Scrace)

The 1894 map has the lines from Cannon Street at the top; Charing Cross at the bottom and London Bridge on the right. Borough Market Junction is to the right of the triangle, within feet of the grounds of St. Saviour's Church (Southwark Cathedral since 1905). Quadrupling between London Bridge and Cannon Street was completed by WWI. The turntable on the right gave access to the locomotive shed, both of which became redundant in 1926. The signal box shown to be partly over the other turntable was Cannon Street No. 2 Box, which was in use until 27th June 1926. This turntable was probably added when the bridge was widened in 1892. In recent years, the left part of the triangle has been used by empty stock running via the Metropolitan Spur or to the electrified berthing sidings on the site of the former Southwark Depot.

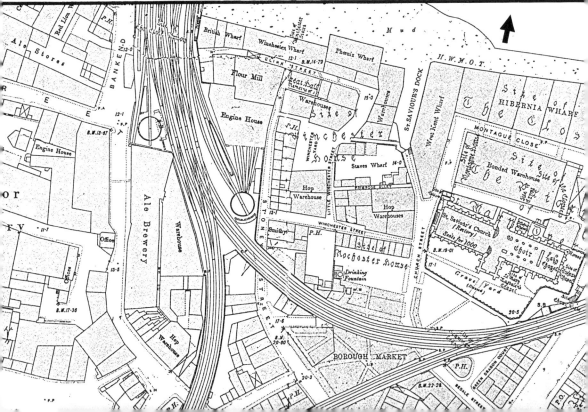

BOROUGH MARKET JUNCTION

26. Viewed from the cab of a train from Charing Cross in 1955, Borough Market Junction Box can be seen to have a window cleaning balcony, unlike many rural SER boxes. Beyond the bridge over Borough High Street, a locomotive waits with empty stock for one of the termini. (R.C.Riley)

27. The box was variously described as the busiest on the SR; in Britain or in the world and it was double manned for much of the time. Its small frame of miniature levers belies its importance. To reduce junction occupation, often two up and two down Cannon Street trains would be signalled simultaneously. Control of the junction was from London Bridge Panel from 16th April 1976. (J.Scrace)

For centuries, Southwark was an important destination for merchandise and passengers. There is much evidence of this on the 1907 map, which shows numerous warehouses, many for hops, and the Borough Market, for fruit and vegetables. The names of the yards of the many inns are shown on the left. Some of these were the terminating point of the stage coaches and two of them are marked as parcel depots for northern railway companies. The George Yard was used by the Eastern Region of BR until the mid-1950s. St Thomas's Hospital was on the north side of St. Thomas's Street and a small part of their property was bought in 1833 for the construction of the first railway terminus. The SER required more of the hospital in order to extend westwards but were obliged to buy the entire property at the massive price of £296,000. A new hospital was built, beyond Westminster Bridge, and the railway acquired some unwanted buildings, marked "Railway Offices" on the map. (The SR used them for CM & EE after WWII). The adjacent St Thomas's Church still contains an historic and primitive operating theatre, thanks to the intervention of the SER in the hospital development. Over the road, the 1722 hospital of Thomas Guy remained unaffected

LONDON BRIDGE

by the traumas of railway expansion. In the station, the LBSCR platforms are numbered 1 to 6, although in reality this represents twelve platforms. The SECR occupies the northern part of the station, comprising both through and terminal roads. No less than four streets are shown to pass under the station. Three and not four tracks passed over Borough High Street at this time.

The original L & G terminus had six tracks but these were insufficient when L & C trains commenced running. A separate station, on the north side, was soon built for the latter. To reduce conflicting movements on the approaches (which were quadrupled on 10th May 1842), the companies exchanged stations in 1844. New joint buildings were completed in 1845 and further expansion resulted in the erection of a new terminus for the SER, seen in the background in 1851.

28. A postcard from the turn of the century has the boundary between the SER and LBSCR stations just left of the centre. In 1850, the LBSCR added a six- platform station to the south of that existing, behind the Terminus Hotel - right. (Lens of Sutton)

29. Women were employed during WWI on a variety of railway work. The tall girl is pumping water to the boy who is filling the lavatory tank, while another is operating the gigantic vacuum cleaner. There is a rare glimpse of the roof which covered the low level SECR platforms prior to the fourth track to Borough Market Junction being added. The front boundary of the roof is shown by a dotted line on the 1907 map, but the track arrangements were different then. (Lens of Sutton)

30. A view east from the SER high-level platforms show class D 4-4-0 no. 733 entering no. 2. The SECR's low level platforms are behind the railings and beyond them is the LBSCR's station, with its massive water tank. The SECR's low level platforms were numbered 1 to 4 and the high level ones 1 to 7, south to north, whereas the LBSCR's were 1 to 11, north to south. (D.Cullum coll.)

31. On the left is the boundary wall of the LBSCR station which was impenetrable until a footway was cut in it in 1928, when the platforms were renumbered 1 to 22, from the north. This picture shows a single footbridge linking the high and low level platforms. The centre through road was numbered 5 by the SR and was often used for holding northbound goods trains. (P.Rutherford)

32. Colour light and semaphore signals coexist (left) as the new all electric signal box (right of centre) is prepared to take over from six other boxes (including B Box, straddling the tracks) on 17th June 1928. Note the lofty water treatment plant. (D.Cullum coll.)

33. Ex-LMS 3F 0-6-0T no. 47435 rises up the 1 in 103 gradient into platform 7, with freight from Hither Green destined for the Midland Region via Farringdon on 13th March 1957. No. 5 road had been removed in 1952. (R.C.Riley)

34. The signalman's view on 14th May 1959 includes no. S5207, bound for Gravesend from platform 4 which was then signalled for reversible running. The cranes on the skyline served shipping in the Pool of London and were soon to become part of transport history. (R.C.Riley)

35. The covered footbridges link the former SER platforms but neither are shown on the 1907 map, when all passengers had to pass the front of the station when changing trains. The roofs over the subway ramps to platforms 1 to 7 are visible on the left. The origin of the bomb battered building becomes clear when comparing this with picture no. 28. (British Rail)

36. Between platforms 7 and 8 was The Mount, a short platform for the exclusive use of mailbags. This photograph shows GPO vans at the loading bay. The sharp curve at the far end of platform 7 added to the problems of steam locomotives restarting a train on the steep gradient. (E.Wilmshurst)

37. The station was almost completely rebuilt in 1973-77 at a cost of over £9m. Most platforms were renumbered and the two clear-view footbridges were replaced with this dreary claustrophobic structure. Otherwise, access and comfort were greatly improved. The train at platform 4 is the 12.33 Charing Cross to Dartford via Greenwich on 26th November 1985, by which time the dockside cranes had been replaced by the constructional variety. (C.Wilson)

Through platform working since 1976.		
1	Cannon Street	Down
2	Cannon Street	Reversible
3	Cannon Street	Up
4	Charing Cross	Reversible
5	Charing Cross	Reversible
6	Charing Cross	Up
(7)	Up passenger loop line	

38. To mark the 150th anniversary of the opening of the L&GR, an exhibition was held at Cannon Street during the weekend of 23rd August 1986. There were 153 stands and numerous items of unusual rolling stock. The station is normally closed at weekends and so a shuttle service of the latest electric stock was operated to Charing Cross. A shuttle of vintage stock was run to London Bridge and is seen entering platform 2. (A.Dasi-Sutton)

SPA ROAD

39. From 8th February until 14th December 1836, a station here was the temporary terminus of the line from Deptford. Thereafter trains called by request at "a low platform, one yard wide". This was closed at the end of 1838 and a new station, with a waiting room, opened on 30th October 1842. It was rebuilt again in 1845 and yet again, further down the line, in 1867. This last station is seen, from the north, prior to final closure on 15th March 1915. (Lens of Sutton)

A map showing the location of Southwark Park Station appears under picture 24 in our *London Bridge to East Croydon* album, which also contains other photographs and diagrams of London Bridge Station.

The 1916 edition shows that island platforms were provided, on the SECR lines only. Spa Road passes under the tracks, to the left of the station.

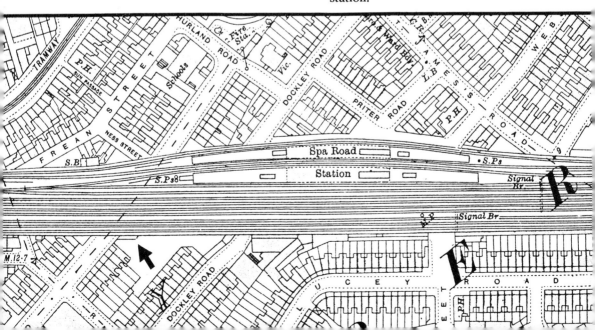

SOUTHWARK PARK

40. The platforms were on the SECR tracks only and were in use from 1st October 1902 until 15th March 1915, being situated close to Corbetts Lane Junction. This view towards London Bridge shows the LBSCR main lines, the SECR up starting signal, Corbett's Lane Box and the roof of Rotherhithe Road Carriage Depot. A station named Commercial Docks had been in use near this site between 1856 and 1866. (D.Cullum coll.)

NORTH KENT EAST JUNCTION

41. This was the principal junction of the SECR in the London area, being at the divergence of the Greenwich and Lewisham lines. An SER style box is seen in front of the elevated one which replaced it in about 1900. This in turn was succeeded in 1929 by one spanning the tracks and controlling colour light signals. (Lens of Sutton)

The pre-grouping diagram shows the line from Bricklayers Arms diverging at Bricklayers Arms Junction, which the SR renamed North Kent West Junction. "East" was added to North Kent Junction at that time.

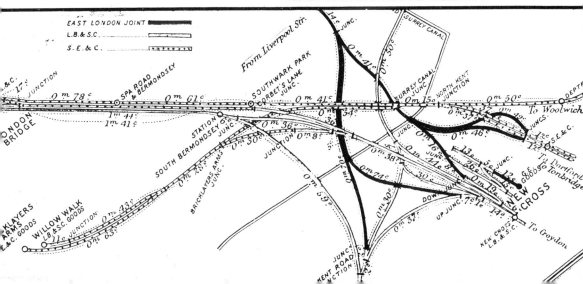

DEPTFORD

42. The station was the eastern terminus from 8th February 1836 until the line was extended to Greenwich on 24th December 1838. This drawing from 1840 illustrates the composite iron and stone bridge chosen by the parish and not the L&GR. (D. Cullum coll.)

The 1st edition of 1869 marks the engine and carriage sheds, which had been enlarged in 1842. Initially, stock was kept under the arches and hauled up an inclined plane. This is shown as the line running south from the turntable.

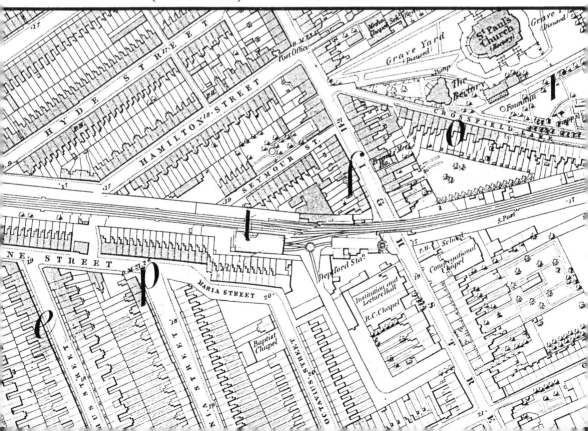

43. The turret on the left was the unusual station entrance, opened in March 1842. The platforms were extended over the High Street. The station was rebuilt in 1904 and again in 1927, the bridge being replaced in December 1963. (Lens of Sutton)

44. An eastward view in 1968 includes fragments of the L&GR buildings on the right. Locomotive repairs continued at Deptford until July 1845, the workshops then being used for wagon construction until 1846, when the task was transferred to Ashford.
(J. N. Faulkner)

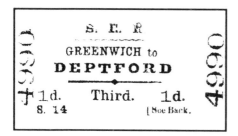

S. E. R

GREENWICH to
DEPTFORD

1d.　Third.　1d.

S. 14　　　[See Back.

4990

SPA ROAD
TO
LONDON BRIDGE

PARLY THIRD.

London B　　London B

9934

45. Looking west in 1989, we see the structure of mainly SR origin on the site of London's oldest passenger station. Initially, the rails were laid on granite blocks but these were soon replaced by timber sleepers, as the former were so unkind to the rolling stock and to the passengers. (J. Scrace)

47. The key which locked the signals in Greenwich Box had to be obtained from there in order to unlock the lever frame (right) which controlled the bridge bolts. The signal wires were disconnected; the keys knocked out from the chairs; the rails ran out on rollers fitted to the decking; the chair bearing timbers lifted out from above the hinges; the bridge bolts withdrawn and then winching could commence. On 6th October 1962, the boat (mast on the right) was 90 minutes late! The bridge had been opened 223 times in 1961 and was replaced by a 40-ton electrically operated structure in December 1963. (J. J. Smith)

DEPTFORD CREEK BRIDGE

46.   The bridge passes over the River Ravensbourne and each flap was fitted with four struts, each hinged to the stone masonry and running on slides under the decking up to stops, near the centre line.   Although partly counterbalanced by weights on chains, six men were required to operate each winch.
(A. E. Bennett)

GREENWICH

A temporary station west of the town was used from 24th December 1838 until this fine building came into use on 12th April 1840. Behind it were four tracks terminating on a 26ft sector plate (or fan table). Prior to extension of services to Maze Hill in 1878, this building, along with 43 of the brick arches carrying the approach lines, were demolished so that the tracks could be lowered to pass under Greenwich Park.

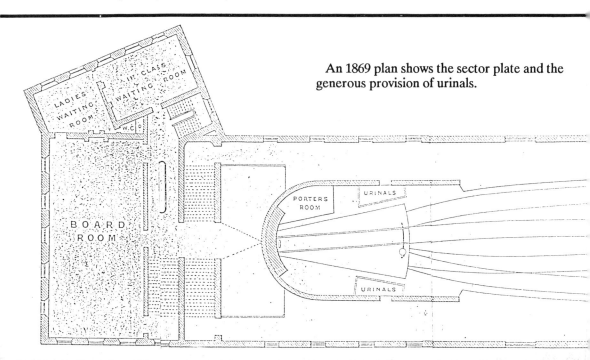

An 1869 plan shows the sector plate and the generous provision of urinals.

48. The line drops at 1 in 66 and then 1 in 89 into the station, the incline being evident as Q class 0-4-4T arrives with a down train on 5th May 1900. Right hand running between London Bridge and Charlton persisted until 26th May 1901. (K. Nunn/LCGB)

The 1895 survey shows a street tramway, which did not become a competitor to the railway until electrified in 1904.

MON.	TUE.	WED.	THU.	FRI.	SAT.

SOUTHERN RAILWAY.
WORKMAN'S   Weekly Ticket.

3 Greenwich to **3**
WATERLOO JUNCTION
AND BACK, 3rd. CLASS 3s. 0d.
Available up to the date stamped
hereon for one journey from and back
to the issuing Station on each day.

FOR CONDITIONS SEE BACK.

MON.	TUE.	WED.	THU.	FRI.	SAT.

264

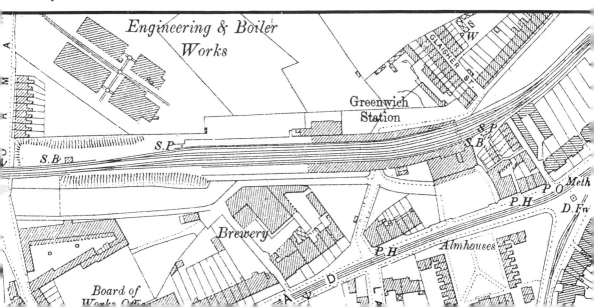

49. An eastward view in July 1920 includes the signal box which replaced the one partially visible in the previous picture. The wide platforms were often crowded with visitors to the town, many of whom visited the beach, indifferent as it is. (D. Cullum coll.)

50. Empty stock from Maze Hill to Rotherhithe Road sidings rumbles through on Whit Monday 1957, behind C class no. 31293. By then, holidaymakers were finding more exotic resorts than Greenwich, such as those on the Kent Coast. (J. J. Smith)

51. The point rodding takes a meandering course where the through roads carried traffic until 5th October 1924. Although rather drab when photographed in 1965, the station still had a good train service. Beyond the foot crossing is the ironwork of a bridge over a minor road. (J. N. Faulkner)

52. This 1989 photograph indicates that the fine structure has been splendidly restored - even the railings have been replaced. Much of the stonework came from the 1840 station. (J. Scrace)

MAZE HILL

53. Trains from Charlton started to run on 1st January 1873 but the link to Greenwich, which was initially single line, was not opened until 1st February 1878. Not only were the buildings timber clad but the platform was also faced with timber. (Lens of Sutton)

The 1916 edition marks two footbridges and two signal boxes, East Box closing on 4th February 1934. The proximity of Greenwich Park is evident.

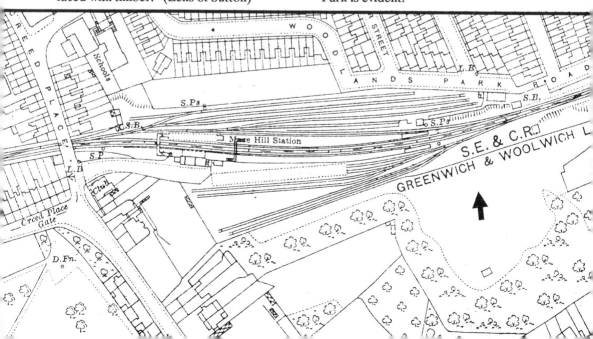

54. Carriage sidings were provided both sides of the station, two of those on the up side being protected by the shelter seen in the background of this 1956 photograph. (H. C. Casserley)

55.   A similar shelter was provided on the down side, seen here protecting Birdcage set no. 519, when the platform canopies and the station buildings were nearing the end of their lives.   (Lens of Sutton)

56. On 4th July 1958, the 9.41am Gravesend to Charing Cross collided with C class 0-6-0 no. 31461, as it was leaving the up sidings with empty coaches for Herne Hill. The ex-SER signal box remained in use until 29th November 1969, by which time the sidings had gone. Upper right are the waterside cranes adjacent to the power station. (British Rail)

57. The reverse curves were necessary to avoid Greenwich Park and to prevent the 450 yd long Greenwich College Tunnel passing directly under what is now the Maritime Museum. The Greenwich Observatory was half a mile south of the line and had the right to stop trains when taking measurements. (Lens of Sutton)

58. The rebuilt station is seen in 1989, by which time flats had been built in that part of Greenwich Park isolated by the road past the station. Part of BR's unwanted trackside linear forest is also visible. (J. Scrace)

WESTCOMBE PARK

SOUTHERN RAILWAY
CHEAP DAY TICKET
Available as advertised
Deptford to
SOUTHAMPTON DOCKS
AND BACK
Third Class
FOR CONDITIONS SEE BACK.
1800   1800

59. Opened as Coombe Farm Lane in 1879, the station now serves a populous residential area. A westward view shows Halstow Road bridge, beyond which there were storage sidings on the down side. The down side structures have been demolished.
(Lens of Sutton)

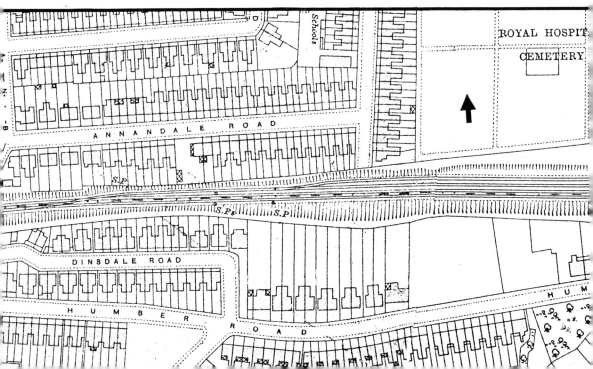

60. A local road, Westcombe Hill, passes under the line beyond the platforms. Between this bridge and that for the Angerstein Wharf branch, there is now another for the dual carriageway of the A102 (M), to the Blackwall Tunnel. (Lens of Sutton)

SOUTHERN RAILWAY.
Issued subject to the Bye-laws, Regulations &
Conditions in the Company's Bills and Notices.

1949 (No.1) Maze Hill to (No.1) 1949
Maze Hill
Deptford
DEPTFORD
Maze Hill
Deptford
THIRD CLASS THIRD CLASS
Fare 2½d Fare 2½d
NOT TRANSFERABLE

The 1916 map shows two berthing sidings in the cutting west of the station, the line to Angerstein Wharf being marked upper right. The signal box closed on 7th February 1926.

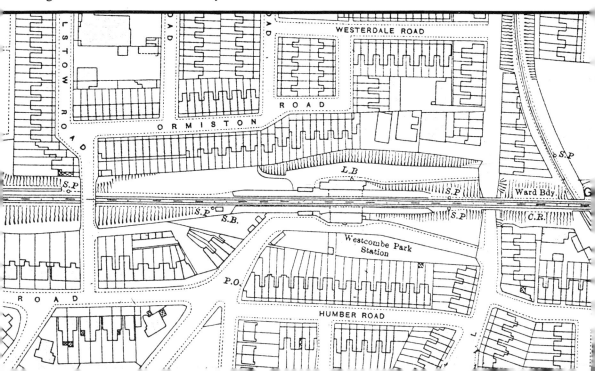

ANGERSTEIN WHARF BRANCH

John Angerstein was a successful businessman from a Russian family and probably the only individual to obtain an Act of Parliament for a railway. Had the mile long branch not passed over a turnpike road, he would have been spared the expense. The 1867 map shows the line emerging from Blackheath Tunnel, lower right, and continuing to Charlton at the top. The 1873 route to Maze Hill passed through the chalk quarry by the limekiln and through the M of COMBE FARM LANE. The branch was leased to the SER from 30th October 1852 until 1898, when it was purchased by them. The company established its signal works in the triangle of the junction and eventually the connection towards London was removed.

61. Looking south-east from the bridge carrying the Westcombe Park - Charlton line over the Angerstein Wharf branch, we see the branch curving left towards the junction and the signal works within the triangle. (A. B. MacLeod)

62. C class no. 31691 stands on the public foot crossing, south of Woolwich Road, with a train from the wharf. The overhead electrification was for use by members of a class of 24 electric locomotives introduced for the Kent Coast electrification in 1959. The equipment was removed in 1976. (D. Cullum)

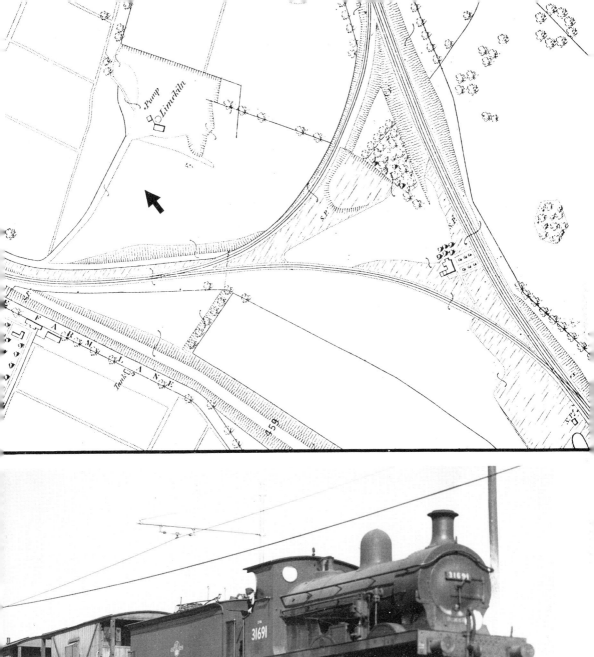

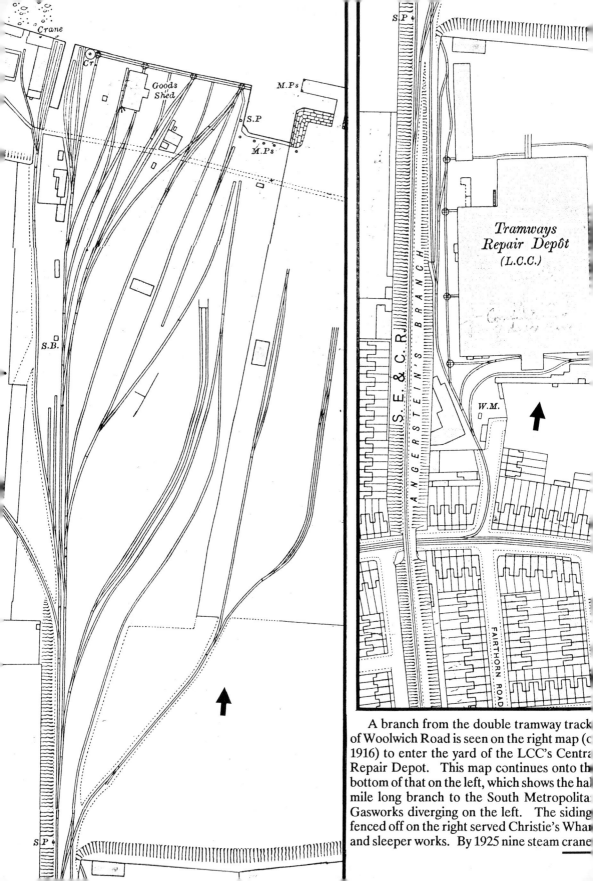

Crane

Cr.

Goods
Shed

M.Ps

S.P

M.Ps

S.B.

S.P

SP

S.E. & C.R. ANGERSTEIN'S BRANCH

*Tramways
Repair Depôt*
(L.C.C.)

W.M.

FAIRTHORN ROAD

A branch from the double tramway track
of Woolwich Road is seen on the right map (o
1916) to enter the yard of the LCC's Centra
Repair Depot. This map continues onto th
bottom of that on the left, which shows the hal
mile long branch to the South Metropolita
Gasworks diverging on the left. The siding
fenced off on the right served Christie's Wha
and sleeper works. By 1925 nine steam crane

63. Esso tank wagons are hauled up the 1 in 215 gradient to the junction, where presumably the obligatory brake van would be added. Feltham tram no. 2150 stands ahead of two earlier cars, while the shunting tractor no. CUC192 manoeuvres on the turntable. Until 1932, shunting was carried out by a Barclay 0-4-0 ST, built in 1904 for Beckton Gas Works. (Lens of Sutton)

64. The last of London's trams ceased to operate on 5th July 1952 but the tracks in the depot were still to be seen from the railway in March 1958. The works were opened in 1909 and were capable of overhauling 1800 trams per annum. The former locomotive shed is lower right. (A. E. Bennett)

were handling 30,000 tons of sleepers over the two and a half miles of track within the works, in addition to the 30,000 tons of telegraph poles produced annually. All this was dispatched by rail, along with 500,000 tons of mixed traffic, which included manure, steel rails, fertilisers, coal, coke, stone, flour, sand, slates, timber and petrol.

65. The line to the East Greenwich Gasworks of the South Eastern Gas Board is on the left as an enthusiasts' railtour runs towards the wharf on 29th March 1958. The Angerstein Wharf branch was still in use in 1990, carrying a heavy traffic in aggregates. (A.E.Bennett)

The 1969 control diagram shows the siding lengths in feet and the wide variety of users. The quadruple track to Charlton is on the right and 600 ft of the connection is shown as electrified. This was by means of a third rail, the overhead area being surrounded by dotted lines.

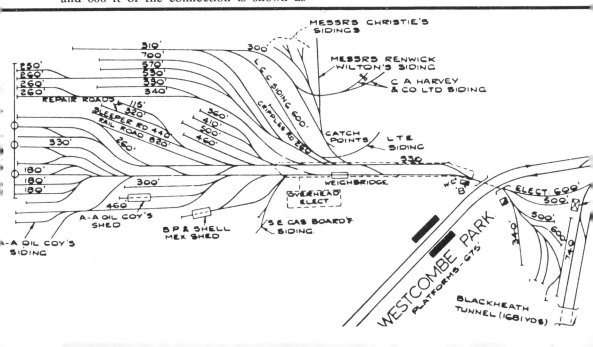

CHARLTON

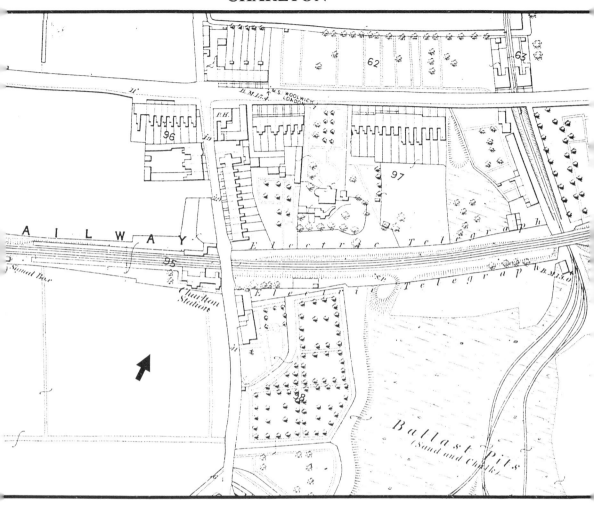

The 1867 survey shows the station to be surrounded by fields and includes an industrial railway running under both the North Kent Line and Woolwich Road. It terminated on a wharf.

66. The station opened with the line and became a junction on 1st January 1873, when the line to Maze Hill came into use. The bay platform for this service is behind the seat. (Lens of Sutton)

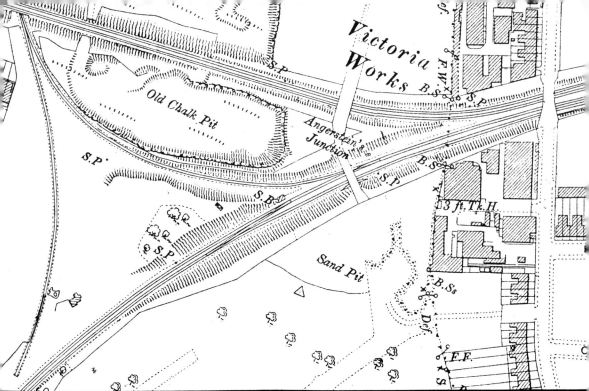

67. Urbanisation of the area in the late 19th century brought an increase in passenger traffic, justifying the generous canopies. Domestic coal traffic increased pro rata. (Lens of Sutton)

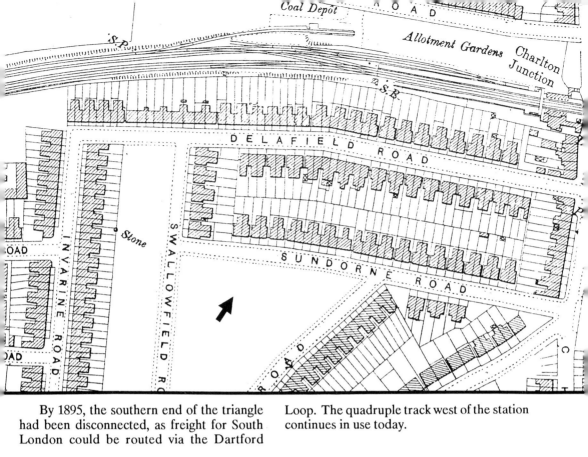

By 1895, the southern end of the triangle had been disconnected, as freight for South London could be routed via the Dartford Loop. The quadruple track west of the station continues in use today.

The 1916 edition indicates the improvements to freight facilities and the extension of the platform canopies.

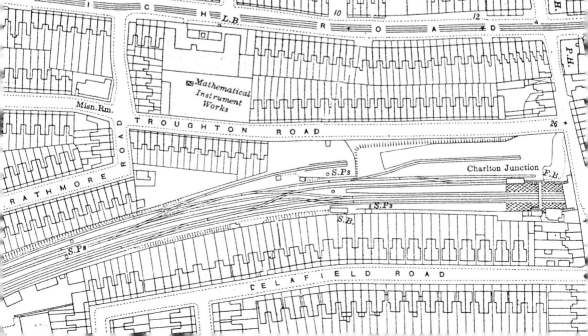

68. This 1962 eastward view is dominated by the electric substation. To the right of it is the loading gauge preceding the two sidings of the goods yard, which closed on 20th May 1963. The signal box was taken out of use on 15th March 1970, when colour light signals were introduced. (British Rail)

69. By 1989, the footbridge was nearer the road bridge and the station buildings were of the CLASP type. In the distance is a trailing crossover and, out of view, is Charlton Lane level crossing. (J. Scrace)

70. Charlton Lane crossing is the nearest to London and is seen on 11th August 1970, as unit no. 5108 emerges from the 154 yd long Charlton Tunnel, bound for Charing Cross. In the distance is Mount Street Tunnel, which is 121 yds in length. Lifting barriers were installed in May 1973. (J. Scrace)

71. Sand Street crossing is shown in February 1960 as an up train rounds the curve from Woolwich Dockyard. The crossing was abolished on 5th August 1969. (J. Scrace)

WOOLWICH DOCKYARD

72. At the east end of the curve seen in the previous picture, a line diverges to serve Woolwich Dockyard. It is only connected to the up track and is seen on 11th July 1961, when a short freight had just left the Dockyard. It was about to reverse over the trailing crossover. (A. E. Bennett)

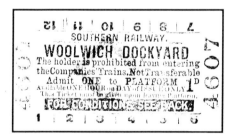

74. A 1960 photograph shows the main entrance on the up side - the down side makes an interesting comparison with the details shown on the map. Redevelopment is in progress in the background, a not uncommon event in the town which has had a Naval dockyard since 1532. (A. E. Bennett)

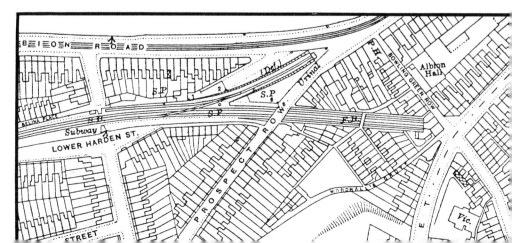

73. The down banner repeater is evident as we look towards the 89 yd Coleman Street Tunnel in 1952. This is followed by George IV Tunnel (238 yds), Calderwood Street Tunnel (58 yds) and Cross Street Tunnel of 134 yds. (D. Cullum)

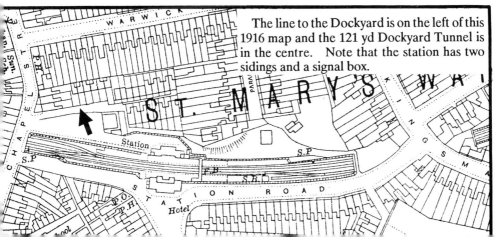

The line to the Dockyard is on the left of this 1916 map and the 121 yd Dockyard Tunnel is in the centre. Note that the station has two sidings and a signal box.

75. The building was damaged by fire on 2nd April 1960 but subsequently repaired. The room on the left was used as a temporary ticket office. (A. E. Bennett)

76. Apart from the provision of NSE nameboards, little had changed when the 12.13 Charing Cross to Gillingham service arrived on 16th June 1989. The platforms had been extended with great difficulty in 1955 to accommodate 10-car trains - greater ingenuity will be required to extend into the tunnel to take twelve coaches. (J. Scrace)

WOOLWICH ARSENAL

77. There is no trace of the original 1849 station, a larger one having been completed in 1906. The spacious forecourt is above the running lines. Tram no. 1487 is bound for Eltham. (Lens of Sutton)

78. After completion of electrification to Dartford in 1926, steam trains for Gravesend and beyond continued to call at Woolwich Arsenal, being the principal station on the route. No. 1274 was one of the successful H class 0-4-4Ts and is showing the headcode for the North Kent and the Nunhead lines to the ex-LCDR termini. (Lens of Sutton)

79. The Arsenal covered 1300 acres and had both narrow and standard gauge internal railway systems. There were up to 28 locomotives on the network at its zenith, four being illustrated in *Industrial Railways of the South-East* (Middleton Press). Two classes were provided, the coach being for officers and staff. (Lens of Sutton)

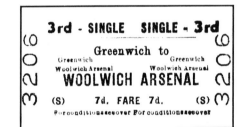

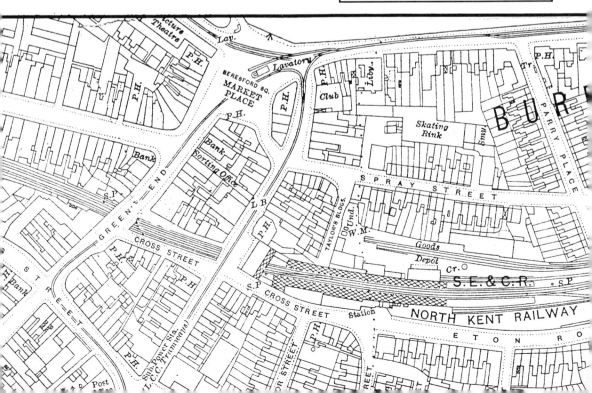

80. The large goods shed was recorded on a grey day in August 1952, along with the inclined roadway leading to the loading dock on the up side, much used in cavalry days. (D. Cullum)

The goods yard contains a weighing machine (W.M.) and a crane (Cr.) which was of 8 ton capacity. The tramways marked on this 1916 edition ran to Abbey Wood, Eltham and into London.

SOUTHERN RAILWAY.
Issued subject to the Bye-laws, Regulations & Conditions in the Company's Bills and Notices.

Royal Arsenal Cooperative Society.
Woolwich Arsenal
or any intermediate Station to
DARTFORD to
MARGATE & BACK

THIRD CLASS
12th. SEPTEMBER 1948
NOT TRANSFERABLE.

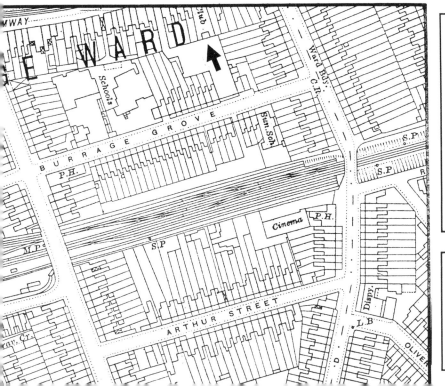

L 0875

SOUTHERN RAILWAY
Issued subject to the Bye-laws, Regulations and Conditions on the Company's Bills and Notices and to the Bye-laws, Regulations and Conditions of the London Passenger Transport Board in force at the time of issue.

DAILY WORKMAN
WOOLWICH DOCKYARD to GREENWICH
Third Class Fare C 5d
Available by Rail or Tram (See back)
NOT TRANSFERABLE

SOUTHERN RAILWAY
DAILY WORKMAN
GREENWICH to
WOOLWICH DOCKYARD
Third Class Fare C 5d
Bell Punch Company, London. 14

1 0875

This return portion is available by Railway or direct Trams Nos. 36, 38 or 40 from Beresford Square to South Street, Greenwich and intermediately. It must be produced on demand for cancellation on the Tram.

14

81. A train of 2 HAL units from Gillingham approaches Woolwich Arsenal box on 2nd April 1956. By then the crossover had been disconnected to allow work on platform lengthening to commence. Closure of the goods yard took place on 17th May 1965 and the box followed on 15th March 1970. (A.E. Bennett)

82. Even in 1958, steam traction was not unknown, being mainly limited to the haulage of newspaper trains, freight and excursionists. This down train on 18th May 1958 is hauled by class D1 no. 31489. (A.E. Bennett)

PLUMSTEAD

83. The station was opened ten years after the line, on 18th July 1859. Photographed after WWII, its appearance belies its importance during that event and during the previous war, when there were over 10,000 employees at the Arsenal, mostly requiring transport daily. The building was still in use in 1989.
(Lens of Sutton)

84. A view towards London from the footbridge in 1952 shows the locomotive water tank and the ground on which sidings once stood. That on the down side was later relaid. Some locomotives for the SR were built at the Arsenal between the wars, to reduce local unemployment. They were N class 2-6-0s, nos. 1826 to 1875. (D. Cullum)

85. A 1963 picture of unit no. 5311 London - bound includes the crossover at the entrance to Plumstead Yard. The down starting signal is obscured, hence the need for the banner repeater. The former bay platform is on the right. (British Rail)

The blank area north of the station is part of the Arsenal, details of which were omitted from all maps on grounds of national security. The rail connection to it is shown left of centre on this 1916 edition. The embankment running diagonally across the right page covers the Southern Outfall Sewers. The A Box (left) was closed on 13th June 1926.

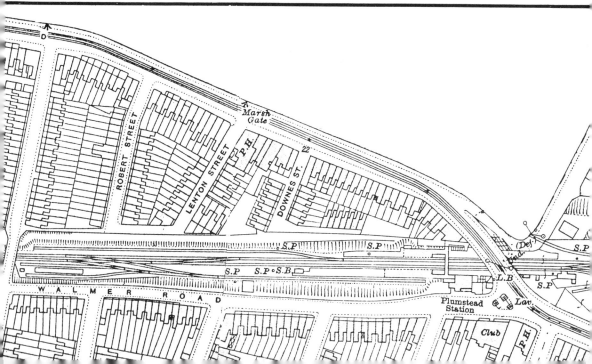

86. No. 33020 leaves the little used yard on 19th June 1989, the siding on the right having once served the Royal Arsenal Cooperative Society. Beyond the yard, there was a halt near Church Manor Way crossing, for use by munition work and open between 1st January 1917 and 31st December 1919. Sidings were laid on the Regent Street Polytechnic playing fields at this time. (J. Scrace)

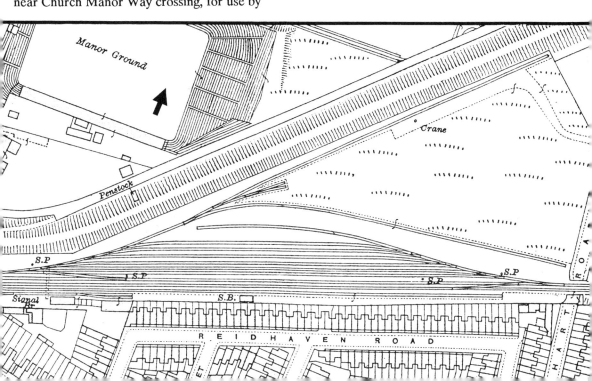

ABBEY WOOD

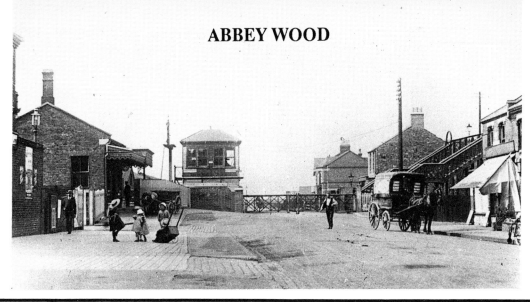

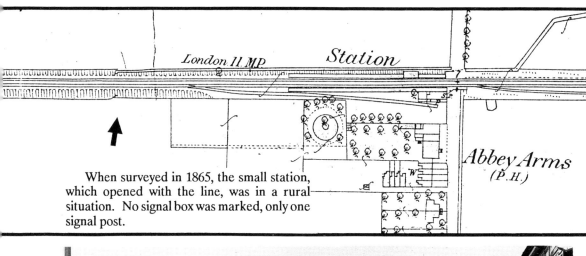

When surveyed in 1865, the small station, which opened with the line, was in a rural situation. No signal box was marked, only one signal post.

87. The station entrance is on the left, under the small canopy. The level crossing remained in use until 13th July 1975, when it was replaced by a bridge. (Lens of Sutton)

89. Two views from June 1989 are included to show the then recently reconstructed station. The goods yard had been in use, behind the up platform, until 5th December 1960 and the LPTB tram depot adjacent to it until 1952. (J.Scrace)

88. An SR style signal is at the far end of this 1962 photograph. The signal box ceased to be a block post on 25th October 1970, after which date it simply controlled the gates until they were abolished. (British Rail)

90. Use of modern ecclesiastical architectural features seems appropriate in the vicinity of the ancient abbey site. The remains of Lesnes Abbey are within 500 yards of the station, on the edge of woodland of the same name. (J. Scrace)

BELVEDERE

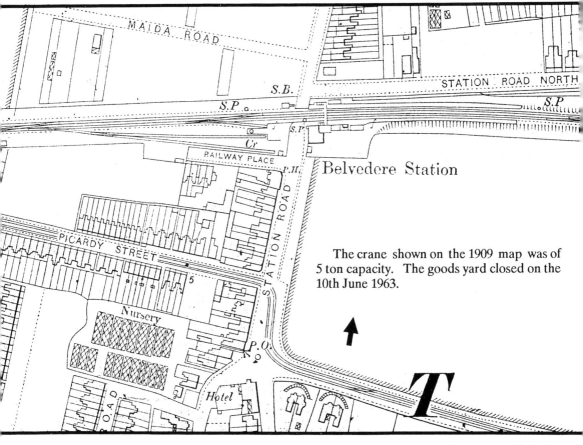

Belvedere Station

The crane shown on the 1909 map was of 5 ton capacity. The goods yard closed on the 10th June 1963.

91. A rural scene is depicted with fields in the background and milk churns waiting for an up train. The station was opened in March 1859 and had a peaceful existence until being severely bombed in April 1941. (Lens of Sutton)

92. Taken on a misty day in January 1956, this picture shows the new signal box under construction, adjacent to the goods yard on the left. (British Rail)

93. A 1965 photograph from the down platform illustrates the facilities provided after WWII until a CLASP building was erected in 1968. The goods yard was behind the signal box, which was downgraded to a gate box on 25th October 1970. Barriers came into use on 25th January 1981 and the level crossing, together with the adjacent one, was abolished on 13th March 1989. (J. N. Faulkner)

ERITH

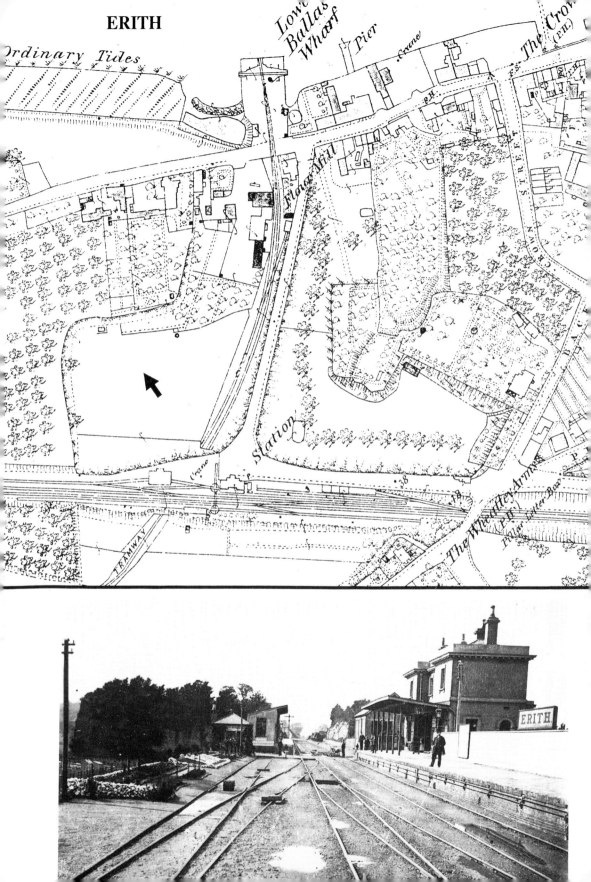

95. Erith Reach is in the left background as the River Thames meanders south to give Erith a natural deep water berthing frontage. The station is about 30ft above sea level, giving the lines to the wharves a substantial gradient. (Lens of Sutton)

The 1865 edition includes the wagon turntables that linked a transverse track between the ends of the platforms.

94. The typical SER plan of staggered platforms connected by a foot crossing was employed. Less typical was the provision of weather protection for passengers. (Lens of Sutton)

96. This level crossing took two single tracks to the ballast wharf across the Erith UDC Tramway rails. The crossing is shown on the left of the previous map, in West Street. The line from Vickers was standard gauge but that from Parish's Loam Quarry was 4ft gauge. (Lens of Sutton)

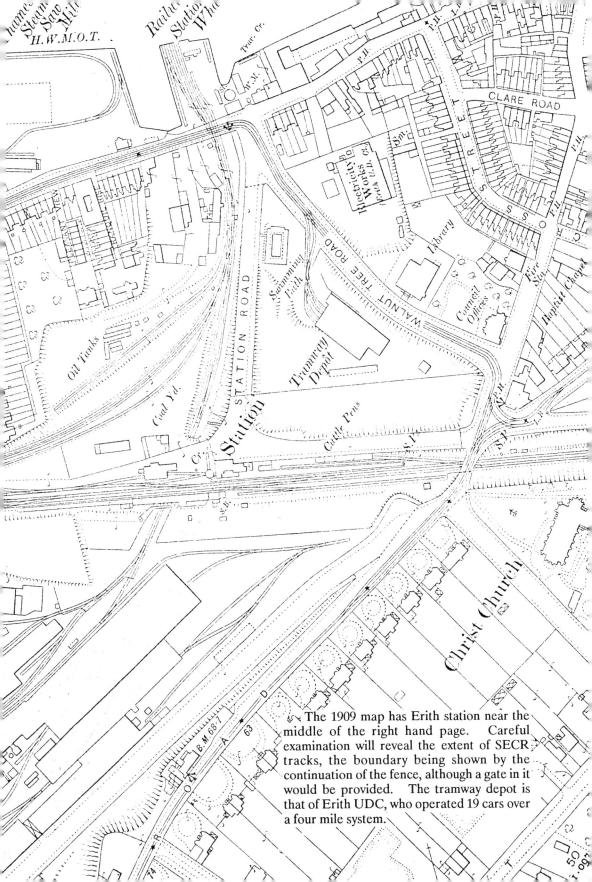

The 1909 map has Erith station near the middle of the right hand page. Careful examination will reveal the extent of SECR tracks, the boundary being shown by the continuation of the fence, although a gate in it would be provided. The tramway depot is that of Erith UDC, who operated 19 cars over a four mile system.

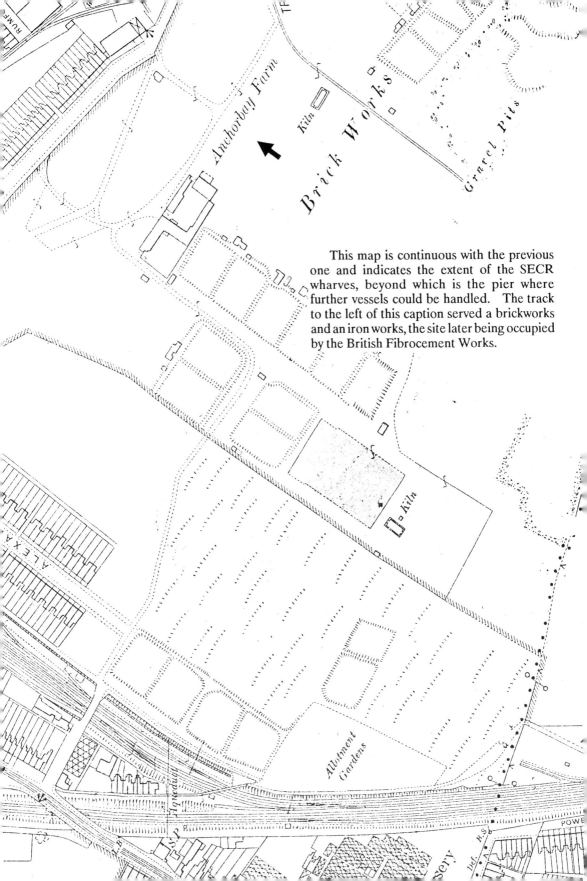

Anchorbay Farm

Kiln

Brick Works

Gravel Pits

This map is continuous with the previous one and indicates the extent of the SECR wharves, beyond which is the pier where further vessels could be handled. The track to the left of this caption served a brickworks and an iron works, the site later being occupied by the British Fibrocement Works.

Kiln

Allotment Gardens

97. Beyond the cattle pens is a grounded coach body of considerable antiquity. Note that the signal posts are tapered, a design also employed by the neighbouring LBSCR. (Lens of Sutton)

98. An up train waits to depart on 8th December 1949 and we see the crowded goods yard, which eventually closed on the 7th October 1968. Two types of ground signal are to be seen. (British Rail)

99. In 1977, platform staggering was still noticeable, despite several platform lengthenings. The line climbs at 1 in 269 through the station and drops at 1 in 323 beyond the bridge. (British Rail)

100. Although disfigured by later additions, the elegance of the original structure was still evident in 1989. In the early years, there were three road sidings beyond Erith - Beadles, Furners and Rutters. (J. Scrace)

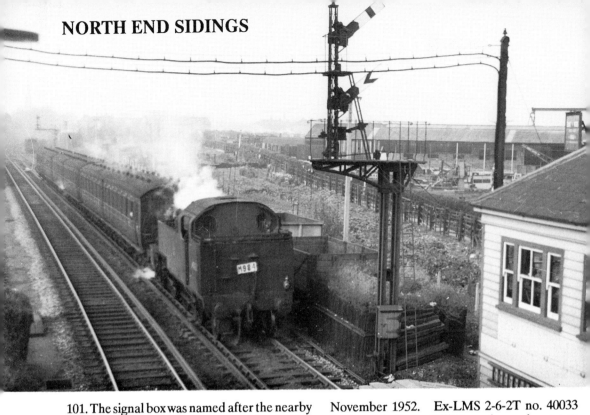

101. The signal box was named after the nearby district of Northend, the connection to the sidings being out of view behind the football special from Hendon to Dartford on 8th November 1952. Ex-LMS 2-6-2T no. 40033 had run via Snow Hill Tunnel, now known as Thameslink, and then very seldom used by passengers. (N. Sprinks)

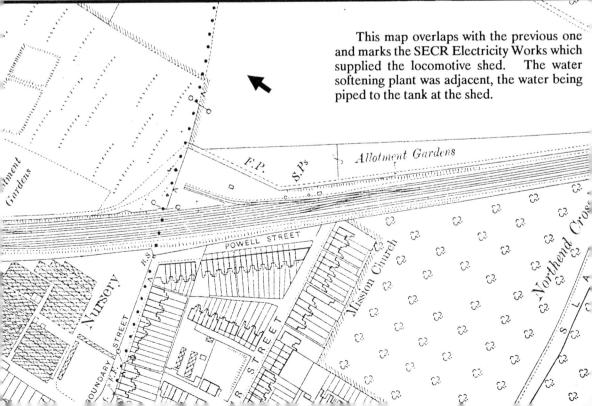

This map overlaps with the previous one and marks the SECR Electricity Works which supplied the locomotive shed. The water softening plant was adjacent, the water being piped to the tank at the shed.

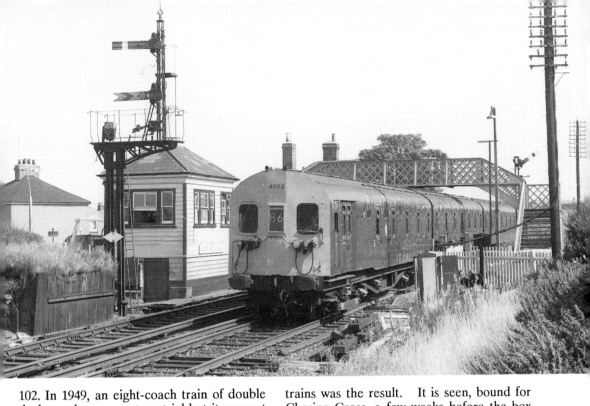

102. In 1949, an eight-coach train of double deck coaches was put on trial but it was not entirely successful owing to the delays caused by so many people having to use each door. The scheme to extend platforms for ten car trains was the result. It is seen, bound for Charing Cross, a few weeks before the box became a crossing box only on 25th October 1970. (J. Scrace)

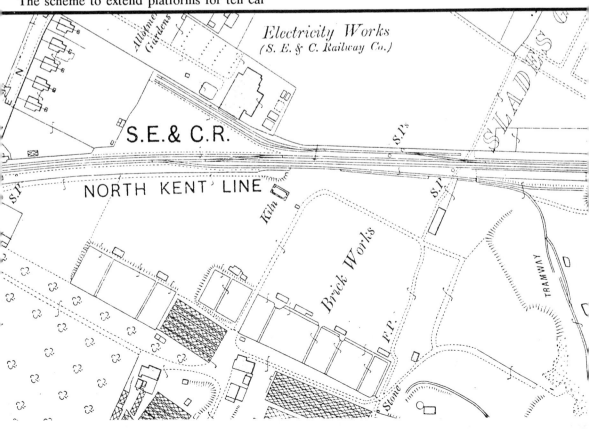

SLADE GREEN

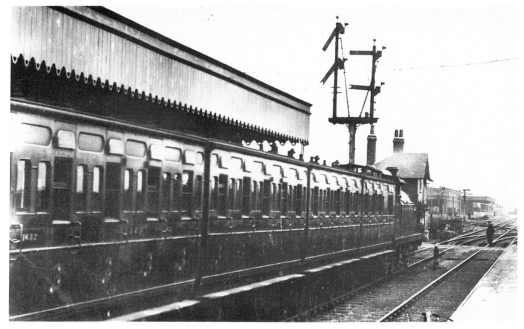

103. The down train is signalled for Dartford, as the close coupled coaches move towards the junction with the Bexleyheath line.   In the distance is the 1901 locomotive shed. (Lens of Sutton)

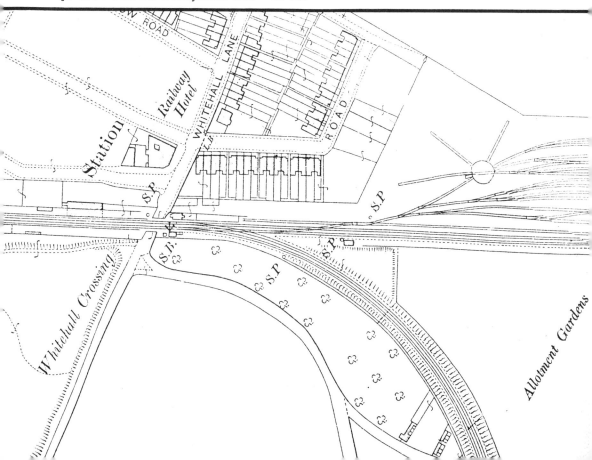

104. The crossing cottage pre-dates the station which was not opened until 1st July 1900, making it the youngest on the route. The brick tower in this 1966 northward view was a late addition to the signal box and housed a toilet. (British Rail)

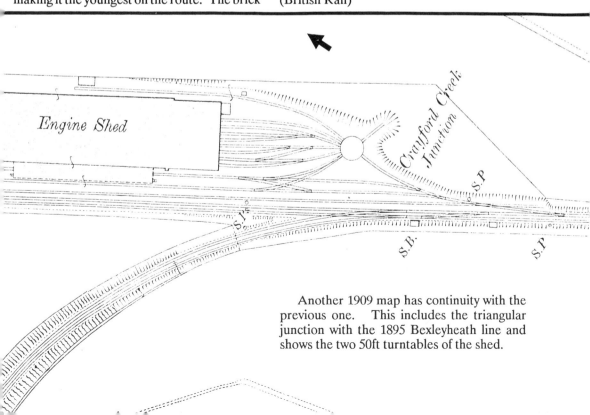

Engine Shed

Crayford Creek Junction

Another 1909 map has continuity with the previous one. This includes the triangular junction with the 1895 Bexleyheath line and shows the two 50ft turntables of the shed.

105. Class 455/8 units were not in regular use when no. 5842 passed through at 13.12 on 21st October 1986. It was travelling empty from East Wimbledon to Slade Green Depot.

Slades Green was the name once used but the final S was officially dropped on 1st August 1953. (D. Brown)

106. With tea can to the fore, diesel-electric no. 58009 was an unusual sight as it left Slade Green on 24th October 1986 with empties from Northfleet to Toton Old Bank. This service normally ran via the Dartford Loop but was diverted due to a weak bridge near Lewisham. (D. Brown)

107. Two class 33s creep into the station on 19th June 1989 and pass over the site of the level crossing (closed 25th January 1971) and the well illuminated Slade Green Junction. The berthing sidings within the triangle and the extension to the old locomotive shed are also visible. (J. Scrace)

SLADE GREEN DEPOT

108. The shed was completed in 1901 and had a two-road repair workshop inside the doors on the left and a long coal stage, beneath the

shelter on the right. Alongside it were three water columns. (Lens of Sutton)

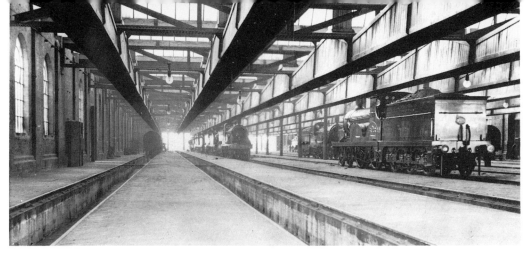

109. The shed could house 110 locomotives and was intended to reduce pressure on the crowded London sheds at Bricklayers Arms and Battersea. (Lens of Sutton)

110. A transitional view of the south end shows conductor rails and one EMU ready for the displacement of steam in 1926. The water tank had a capacity of 150,000 gallons. (Lens of Sutton)

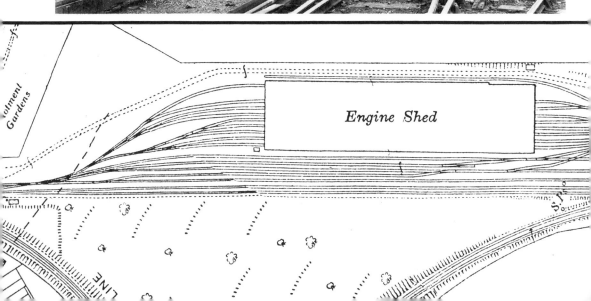

Engine Shed

111. Crayford Creek Junction Box is in the distance in this 1949 photograph of the north end of the inspection shed. The raised part above the workshops originally housed two 5 ton travelling cranes. (British Rail)

112. The repair shed was extensively clad with asbestos and is seen from a passing train on 10th March 1957, with ex LBSCR class H2 no. 32425 in use as a temporary boiler. (A. E. Bennett)

The 1933 map incorrectly described the buildings, as they had been used for electric multiple units since 1926. The shed on the right was erected in 1925 as a repair depot, the old engine shed becoming an inspection shed.

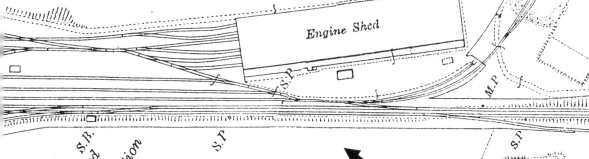

Engine Shed

S.B. Crayford Creek Junction

113. Crayford Creek Junction Box controlled the junction between the North Kent and Bexleyheath lines, until colour light signals, operated from Dartford Panel, came into use on 1st November 1970. (J. Scrace)

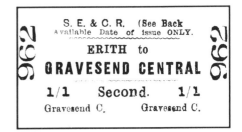

114. Crayford Spur A Box closed on the same day, the box being at the north end of the triangular junction with the Dartford Loop. The spur came into traffic on 11th October 1942. (J. Scrace)

115. Dartford Junction Box closed on the same day as the two previously illustrated, and is shown on 1st September 1970, with unit no. 5152 coming off the Dartford Loop and no. E6015 to the right. One up and two down tracks ran parallel from here to Dartford, the centre one now being reversible. (J. Scrace)

DARTFORD

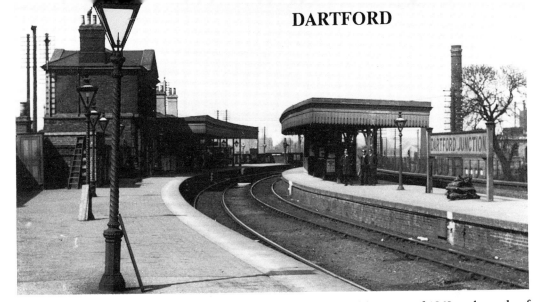

116. The entrance was through the main building on the up platform of the station, which opened with the line on 30th July 1849. Dartford was an important industrial and trading centre long before the railway arrived. (Lens of Sutton)

The 1st edition map of 1869 at the scale of 6" to 1 mile reveals the small size of the country town at that time. The line from Woolwich is upper left and the navigable River Darent is also at the top. For details of this please see *Kent & East Sussex Waterways* (Middleton Press).

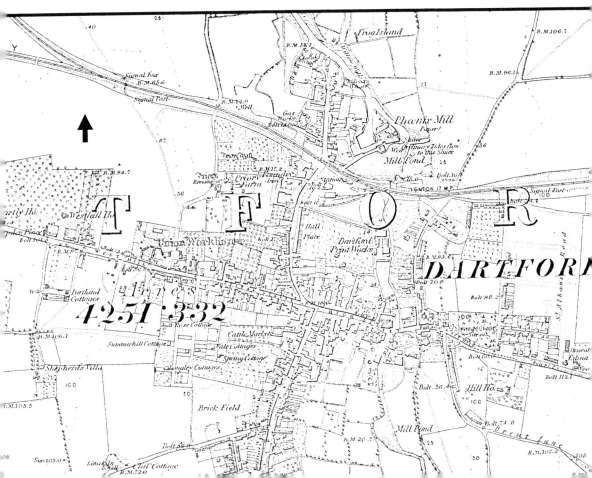

117. Looking towards London in 1955, it is evident from the signals that up trains could be started from any of the platforms. In the peak hours, an intensive service was operated with difficulty from only three platforms. No. 1 Box was abolished on 13th June 1954, in connection with the 10 car train scheme. (D. Cullum)

118. A 1971 photograph reveals the condition of the station just prior to the major rebuilding which resulted in four platforms being available from 5th August 1973. (D. Cullum)

119. The brick part of the station is to the right of the camera, in this September 1971 view. The SER had not been noted for its generosity regarding facilities for passengers. (British Rail)

120. The 1972 reconstruction resulted in less congestion for passengers and greater flexibility for operating staff. The new entrance for this busy station is seen in 1989, when passenger traffic was increasing at about 4% per annum. (J. Scrace)

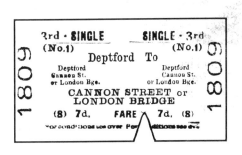

3rd · **SINGLE**   **SINGLE** · 3rd
(No.1)   (No.1)
Deptford To
Deptford   Deptford
Cannon St.   Cannon St.
or London Bge.   or London Bge.
CANNON STREET or
LONDON BRIDGE
(8) **7**d.   **FARE**   **7**d. (8)

1809

Dartford

Easebourne Lane, Midhurst. West Sussex. GU29 9AZ
(0730) 813169

BRANCH LINES

BRANCH LINES TO MIDURST
BRANCH LINES AROUND MIDHURST
BRANCH LINES TO HORSHAM
BRANCH LINES TO EAST GRINSTEAD
BRANCH LINES TO ALTON
BRANCH LINE TO HAYLING
BRANCH LINE TO SOUTHWOLD
BRANCH LINE TO TENTERDEN
BRANCH LINES TO NEWPORT
BRANCH LINES TO TUNBRIDGE WELLS
BRANCH LINE TO SWANAGE
BRANCH LINES TO LONGMOOR
BRANCH LINE TO LYME REGIS
BRANCH LINE TO FAIRFORD
BRANCH LINE TO ALLHALLOWS
BRANCH LINES AROUND ASCOT
BRANCH LINES AROUND WEYMOUTH
BRANCH LINE TO HAWKHURST
BRANCH LINES AROUND EFFINGHAM JNC

SOUTH COAST RAILWAYS

CHICHESTER TO PORTSMOUTH
BRIGHTON TO EASTBOURNE
RYDE TO VENTNOR
EASTBOURNE TO HASTINGS
PORTSMOUTH TO SOUTHAMPTON
SOUTHAMPTON TO BOURNEMOUTH
ASHFORD TO DOVER
BOURNEMOUTH TO WEYMOUTH

SOUTHERN MAIN LINES

HAYWARDS HEATH TO SEAFORD
EPSOM TO HORSHAM
CRAWLEY TO LITTLEHAMPTON
THREE BRIDGES TO BRIGHTON
WATERLOO TO WOKING
VICTORIA TO EAST CROYDON
TONBRIDGE TO HASTINGS
EAST CROYDON TO THREE BRIDGES
WOKING TO SOUTHAMPTON
WATERLOO TO WINDSOR
LONDON BRIDGE TO EAST CROYDON

COUNTRY RAILWAY ROUTES

BOURNEMOUTH TO EVERCREECH JNC
READING TO GUILDFORD
WOKING TO ALTON
BATH TO EVERCREECH JUNCTION
GUILDFORD TO REDHILL
EAST KENT LIGHT RAILWAY
FAREHAM TO SALISBURY
BURNHAM TO EVERCREECH JUNCTION
REDHILL TO ASHFORD

LONDON SUBURBAN RAILWAYS

CHARING CROSS TO DARTFORD

STEAMING THROUGH

STEAMING THROUGH KENT
STEAMING THROUGH EAST HANTS
STEAMING THROUGH SURREY
STEAMING THROUGH WEST SUSSEX
STEAMING THROUGH THE ISLE OF WIGHT
STEAMING THROUGH WEST HANTS

OTHER RAILWAY BOOKS

WAR ON THE LINE
GARRAWAY FATHER & SON
LONDON CHATHAM & DOVER RAILWAY
INDUSTRIAL RAILWAYS OF THE S. EAST
WEST SUSSEX RAILWAYS IN THE 1980S

OTHER BOOKS

MIDHURST TOWN THEN & NOW
EAST GRINSTEAD THEN & NOW

WALKS IN THE WESTERN HIGH WEALD

MILITARY DEFENCE OF WEST SUSSEX
SUSSEX POLICE FORCES

SURREY WATERWAYS
KENT AND EAST SUSSEX WATERWAYS